ELLEN

The girl with two angels

D1316895

Mabel R. Miller

Pacific Press® Publishing Association
Nampa, Idaho
Oshawa, Ontario, Canada

Edited by Jerry D. Thomas
Designed by Dennis Ferree
Cover art by Marika Hahn
Inside illustrations by Linda Hawkins
Typeset in New Century Schoolbook 14/17

Additional copies of this book are available by calling
 1-800-765-6955 or by visiting www.adventistbookcenter.com.

Library of Congress Cataloging-in-Publication Data
Miller, Mabel R. (Mabel Robinson), 1920-
        Ellen : the girl with two angels/Mabel R. Miller.
            p. cm.
    ISBN 13: 978-0-8163-1325-9
    ISBN 10: 0-8163-1325-3 (alk. paper)
    1.   White, Ellen Gould Harmon, 1827-1915.
 I. Title.
 BX6193.W5M48 1996
 286.7'092—dc20
 [B]   95-26698
                                          CIP
                                          AC

10 11 • 8 7

Contents

1. Little Ellen's Home   5

2. Bossy Gets Stuck   13

3. What One Stone Did   21

4. Jesus Is Coming!   31

5. Sad and Disappointed   41

6. Good News From Heaven   47

7. The Day Ellen Ran Away   53

8. Messenger for God   61

9. Ellen Sees the New Earth   67

10. Every Drop of Water in the Ocean   77

11. Ellen's Second Angel   87

CHAPTER

1

Little Ellen's Home

"I have something special to tell you this morning," Papa Harmon said from his chair at the head of the long table. The four Harmon children on each side of the table stopped eating to listen. Papa smiled at Mama at the other end of the table. "But I'll save the surprise until breakfast is over."

When their bowls and plates were cleared, the children waited patiently. They knew what would come next. Papa opened his Bible and read some verses, then prayed for the family, especially for each of his children.

After he said, "Amen," he looked around at his big family and smiled. "When you finish your chores this morning, you may go play at the old Indian fort."

Ellen, four years old, looked at Mama, who smiled and nodded. Ellen came off her chair so fast she nearly fell, then started jumping up and down. As she jumped she yelled, "We'll play Indians. Ooh lah lah lah, ooh lah lah lah!" Right away, her twin, Elizabeth, jumped down and joined the pretend war dance.

Long before, the settlers at their tiny village of Gorham had built the fort to protect themselves from Indians. The children heard many stories about the brave pioneers looking for new homes. They also heard about the brave Indians who thought they had to protect themselves from all the palefaces invading their homeland.

Father smiled at their excitement. "I'll call you when it's time to come home," he said.

The eight Harmon children hurried to do their jobs so they could go play.

Six-year-old Robert washed the dishes, swept the porch, and fed the dog. While he did that, Sarah, who was nine, fed and watered the chickens and gathered the eggs. Mary, eleven years old, made all the beds and swept the upstairs.

John, tall and strong at fifteen, ran to the barn and put fresh hay in the stalls for the cow and horses. Then he pumped water from the well for the animals and carried several large buckets to the kitchen.

Harriet, nearly grown at seventeen, picked a basket of peas, shelled them for dinner, and scrubbed potatoes to put into the oven.

Caroline, the oldest at nineteen, decided she was too old to play at the fort, so she stayed home to mend socks, iron clothes, and help with dinner.

The twins, Ellen and Elizabeth, were four and had the easiest jobs of all. They dried the dishes and set the table for dinner.

Everyone hurried, but Ellen and Elizabeth finished first. While they waited for their big brothers and sisters, they found some long strips of paper. "Let's make Indian headdresses!" Ellen said. They colored Indian designs on the paper and fitted them around each other's heads.

"Now all we need are some feathers,"

Elizabeth decided. "Let's use those turkey feathers we saved!" With the big turkey feathers stuck into their bands, the twins felt like real Indians.

When the seven children reached the park around the fort, no one wanted to be a settler. "Let's all be Indians," John suggested. "Remember, Indians can walk silently through the forest."

Hiding behind trees and bushes as they sneaked toward the fort, Ellen and Elizabeth tried to move as quietly as possible. The longer they played and ran, the hotter and thirstier Ellen felt. *Maybe this game isn't as much fun as I remembered*, she thought.

Finally, the children reached the fort where white people had hidden long ago. And to their surprise, they found a real paleface there!

"Caroline!" Ellen cried. "You surprised us!" Then she noticed the pail in her sister's hand. "And you brought us water to drink!"

Ellen thought she couldn't wait for her turn, but as soon as Elizabeth drank, Caroline gave her a big dipperful. The seven Indians lay on the fresh green grass, resting and drinking until all the good water disappeared.

Lying there in the warm sunshine made Ellen sleepier and sleepier. Just as her eyes were closing, she heard a faraway voice calling.

"Dinner's ready."

"Papa!" Ellen said suddenly. "Papa's calling. Let's go!" Ellen jumped up, and they hurried home, hungry for some of Mama's good food.

The Harmon family lived happily on the farm for several more years. Then one morning, Papa had another announcement to make. "I want you children to pack your things into the boxes I'm making," he said. "We're moving into a town twelve miles from here. We'll still live in Maine, but our new home is in a town called Portland."

Move? Ellen could hardly imagine that. She loved the farm. "Why, Papa? Why do we have to leave our farm?" she asked as tears began to squeeze out of her eyes. "I love Bossy and the horses. I love the dogs too."

Papa held his little girl close. "You won't have to give them up, Ellen. We'll take them with us. But we must move. You know what

Mama and I do to earn money, don't you?"

Ellen nodded. She'd watched Mama and Papa making hats ever since she could remember.

"Well," Papa said, "there aren't very many people living out here in the country, so we can't sell enough hats. We need to sell lots of hats to buy food for our family. How many people are in our family?"

Ellen thought a moment and held up eight fingers with a satisfied grin. But Papa shook his head. "There are eight children, but Mama and I are part of the family too. There are ten people in our family. It takes a lot of money to buy food and clothes for all ten of us. Besides, you children have to go to school. You and Elizabeth are six now, Ellen, so you'll be starting school this fall."

Papa nodded as he thought out loud. "We have to move to town where more people will buy hats, Ellen, so we'll have enough money to care for our large family." He slid her to her feet on the floor. "Now go start packing your things."

The thought of going to school filled Ellen with excitement. She'd been wanting to go to school for a long time. Her tears disappeared. *Living in a town won't be so bad,* she decided, *since Papa promised we could bring our dogs and cows and horses and chickens.*

Ellen and Elizabeth liked their new home in Portland.

Every Sunday they went to the Methodist church. They loved their new Sunday School teacher, who told them exciting stories about God rescuing His people. They heard how God rescued Daniel from the hungry lions and Shadrach, Meshach, and Abednego from the fiery furnace. The teacher even told them that God's Son walked in the burning fire with the three friends. No one was burned. Ellen loved her wonderful God.

More than anything else, Ellen wanted to be a faithful follower of God, just like Daniel and his friends.

God had His eye on little Ellen. He had a big plan for her life.

2

Bossy Gets Stuck

very morning after breakfast, Papa called his family together and read from the Bible. Then they knelt down while he asked God to love and care for each of his eight children.

One of Ellen's chores each morning was to lead Bossy, their cow, out of the barn and down the road to her pasture. Bossy stayed in the field all day. Trees shaded her from the hot sun, plenty of green grass filled her tummy, and a nearby stream gave her all the water she wanted.

Each afternoon, Ellen walked to find Bossy and bring her back to the barn. Ellen didn't mind, because she loved Bossy like a pet. And Bossy seemed to love Ellen too, since Ellen treated Bossy so kindly.

One afternoon, Ellen couldn't find Bossy. No matter where Ellen looked and how long she called, she didn't hear Bossy's low "*Moooooooo.*" Ellen looked behind the trees. She walked a long way, looking everywhere for the cow.

Could someone have taken her? Ellen wondered. She felt sad, but she didn't go home crying and asking someone to come help her. She just kept looking.

After she'd looked a long time and felt almost too tired to take one more step, she thought she heard a faint sound.

Moooooo!

Ellen straightened her shoulders, turned her head, and listened. She didn't hear it again, but slowly she began to run toward the spot from which the sound had come.

When she reached the creek, down from where she'd been looking, she found Bossy. The cow stood at the edge of the water, with her four feet stuck deep in the mud. Bossy's head hung down as if it were too heavy to lift.

"You must be hungry." Ellen talked kindly to the cow while she picked a handful of the green grass growing beside the creek. She reached out as far as she could and let Bossy eat the grass from her hand.

Ellen picked another handful of grass, but this time, on purpose, she held it too far away for her to reach it.

Oh, how Bossy wanted that delicious grass! She stretched her neck to reach it and tried to lift one foot out of the mud.

Quickly, Ellen grabbed one of the cow's horns with her free hand and shouted, "Come on, Bossy! Come on! You can make it."

Bossy seemed to understand, and as Ellen pulled with all her strength, Bossy did her best too. One by one, those four feet came out of the deep mud. The thick mud gave a loud *SLURCH!* as each foot came out.

"Thank You, God!" Ellen shouted. "Thank You for helping Bossy. And for helping me too."

In minutes, Ellen and Bossy headed back to the barn. Mud covered both of them, but the girl and the cow had never been happier.

One fall morning, the school bell rang.

Ellen and Elizabeth were so excited they nearly ran to their first day of school. Robert, now nine, walked with the twins, and so did Sarah, who was eleven.

As they neared town, the dusty path turned into a sidewalk made from boards. Then they crossed a grassy little park, and there in front of them stood Bracket Street School.

The school rose two stories into the air. The older children's rooms were upstairs, and the younger children studied downstairs. The first three grades met in a big room with long tables and benches. Ellen and Elizabeth found a bench low enough for their feet to touch the floor.

The kindly man teacher sat on a chair on a high platform behind a big desk. When all the children had found benches, he stood up. "We have a few rules you must obey," he said. "We'll have absolutely no whispering in my class. No laughing or moving about, either. Keep your eyes on your books, and you'll have no problems."

Ellen loved school. She especially enjoyed learning to read. The teacher allowed each child to learn at their own speed, so some read through three reading books while others read only one. In only a few months, Ellen and Elizabeth read with the second-graders.

When Ellen and Elizabeth reached third grade, the teacher sent them upstairs to study with the older students.

The Bracket Street School never had enough textbooks for each child, so everyone shared. Sometimes the teacher asked one of the students who read well to read the lesson aloud to the other children while he taught another class.

Soon, he asked Ellen to read the lessons to her classmates. Sometimes the teacher downstairs sent for Ellen to come read to the beginners. Ellen enjoyed this. It kept her busy.

Round-faced Ellen, with her sparkling eyes and rosy cheeks, enjoyed every minute of school. She enjoyed helping the other students, and she also enjoyed playing with her friends at recess and noon.

When school was out, the twins hurried home. They had chores to do. One day, Mama asked Ellen to dust the furniture in the front room. Ellen had planned to go out under the big tree to read for a while. "Why do I have to do everything?" she muttered quietly so Mama wouldn't hear. "I help a lot around here, and this is going to be *my* time." Then she hurried out the door.

A moment later, Mama appeared in the doorway. "Ellen, come back here and tell me what you just said."

Ellen didn't want to. She didn't want Mama to know about her cross words.

"Ellen, please come here." Slowly, Ellen shuffled through the door.

"Tell me right now, Ellen," Mama repeated.

Ellen bowed her head and blushed as she said the spiteful words again. They sounded awful now.

Mama held out her arms to Ellen, and they prayed, asking God to forgive her. Then Ellen did the dusting without being asked again. When she finally was able to read her book in the shade, she enjoyed it because she had obeyed Mama.

Every morning, Ellen remembered to ask Jesus to help her be kind, good, and cheerful.

3

What One Stone Did

Father was taking a trip to Georgia to sell hats. He also had to buy materials to make more hats.

The Harmon family went with him to the Portland Hotel to see him off on the stagecoach. A stagecoach was a beautiful carriage pulled by six horses. The horses ran swiftly, and every few miles the stagecoach stopped to get fresh horses, leaving the first six to rest.

The family listened to hear the stagecoach horn. "Listen!" Robert shouted. "I hear it! It's coming."

Almost at once, the six horses came prancing around the bend in the road pulling a fancy stagecoach, trimmed with gold and yellow. They stopped in front of the hotel. Ellen thought she'd never seen a prettier sight.

The driver jumped from his high seat to the ground. He hurried to the back of the coach and climbed the ladder. Papa handed up his boxes of hats for the driver to store away on top of the stagecoach.

Papa turned to his family and hugged each one, whispering blessings in each ear as he did. The driver had already jumped into his high seat, so Papa hurried inside to his seat. "Help your mother," Papa shouted back as the horses dashed down the road in a cloud of dust.

"Mama, how long will Papa be gone?" Ellen asked when the stagecoach had gone around a bend and disappeared. She swallowed hard to keep the tears from her eyes.

"Honey," Mama said softly, "it's over one thousand miles to Georgia. Papa will be back in maybe two, three, or four months. I know that's a long time, but we'll work together, won't we?"

"Yes, Mama, we will," the children agreed.

The days and weeks passed as the children went to school and helped Mama at home. Ellen and Elizabeth were now nine years old and able to be a big help to their mother. But nothing was the same without Papa.

One afternoon, the twins and a classmate came out of school and started home. Singing, hand in hand, they started across the park.

Suddenly, they heard the angry voice of a thirteen-year-old girl behind them. She was yelling and threatening to hurt them. This frightened the little girls, so they ran as fast as they could.

For a few minutes, they didn't hear the voice, but soon the angry shouts started again, this time closer than before.

Ellen looked back to see how close the angry girl was. At that very moment, the older girl hurled a stone at Ellen, Elizabeth, and her friend. The stone flew through the air and hit Ellen right in the face.

Ellen fell to the ground. The stone had knocked her out. Blood soon covered her face and dress.

The next thing Ellen knew, she awoke in a nearby store where the girls had carried her.

"Let me take you home with my horse and carriage," a kind man offered.

"Thank you," Ellen murmured weakly. "But I'm afraid all this blood will stain your carriage. I feel better now. I can walk."

Elizabeth and the friend put their arms around Ellen, helping her walk. Slowly they walked, step by step by step. But they hadn't gone very far when Ellen fell unconscious again. The girls carried her the rest of the way home.

Ellen lay unconscious for one week, then two, then three long weeks. Doctors came but didn't know how to help Ellen. "She will die," they whispered sadly as they left.

"Dear Lord," Ellen's mother prayed, "please, please don't let my precious Ellen die. Everyone who sees her says she cannot live. Please, heavenly Father, teach me how to care for her."

God answered Mother Harmon's prayer. She had a cradle built big enough to fit Ellen. As she worked around the home, she kept rocking the cradle with her foot. She seemed to hear

God saying, "Keep Ellen's little body moving."

Mother Harmon sang to Ellen. She talked to her even though Ellen never answered. Little Ellen just lay very still, not moving or speaking. Since she didn't eat for three weeks, she grew thinner and thinner. Mother massaged Ellen's legs and arms, trying to keep them warm.

Finally, Ellen began to awaken. She opened her eyes and looked around. She didn't know why she was in bed, feeling so weak. She didn't know why she'd grown so thin. She didn't even remember being hit with the stone. Mama didn't wait for Ellen to remember anything. She hurried to the kitchen and brought her some warm milk. She fed it to Ellen with a teaspoon.

Another month passed before Ellen could even raise her head. During that month, Mama told her all that had happened. "The doctors said that you would die, but I prayed to God. I asked Him to help you, since the doctors couldn't. And He did."

Ellen slowly grew better. One day, the door opened, and in walked Father Harmon.

He'd been gone for three months.

"Papa's home!" Robert shouted. John, Sarah, Mary, and Elizabeth rushed to greet him. He hugged them all, then looked around. "Where's my Ellen with the rosy cheeks?" he asked.

Ellen stood leaning against the wall across the room, afraid to run to him like the others—afraid that she would fall down. When her own papa didn't recognize her, Ellen's heart nearly broke. Then she knew how much she had changed. Pushing the tears back, she tried to smile.

"Here she is, Papa," Elizabeth called, running to her twin's side. In a moment, Ellen felt Papa's strong, tender arms holding her close.

Ellen kept getting stronger. She wanted to go back to school. Mama and Papa knew she wasn't strong enough yet, so they asked her to wait. Month after month, she kept asking to go back to school. She wanted to catch up on her lessons and see her friends again.

Finally, the day came. Ellen could hardly wait to get back to her school desk. But when she tried to read, the words looked all blurred and mixed up. When she tried to write, her hands trembled so badly she could hardly hold the pencil. Her writing looked like scratches.

The teacher asked the girl who had thrown the stone to help Ellen write and to read her lessons to her. The girl seemed sorry she'd hurt Ellen so badly and did her best to help. Ellen never reminded her of what had happened or how badly she'd been hurt.

While Ellen was trying so hard to study, sweat dripped from her forehead, and she became dizzy and faint.

Finally the teacher had to say, "Ellen, dear, you're too sick to be in school. Come back when you get stronger."

Ellen kept asking to go back to school. There were so many things she wanted to learn! Several times she tried to return, but she had to quit, again and again. Finally, Mama, Papa, and her teacher told her she wouldn't be able to finish school, not even the fourth grade.

Ellen had dreamed of growing up and becoming a teacher. Now it would never happen. She was very, very sad. Her friends, who always wanted to be with her when she was pretty and strong, soon forgot all about her.

Ellen felt sad and lonely. She began to think more and more about Jesus. He'd suffered much more than she. And when things got tough, His friends had all deserted Him too. She spent a lot of time talking to Jesus. She felt His love and comfort. Soon, He became her best friend.

CHAPTER

4

Jesus Is Coming!

One day, when the twins were twelve years old, a preacher came to their town. Preacher Miller had learned something exciting from his Bible, and he wanted to share it with everyone everywhere. He traveled around to preach wherever people would listen.

"King Jesus is coming!" he said during his meetings. "He's coming in the clouds of heaven. He's coming soon. Get ready to meet your Saviour."

He held meetings every morning, every afternoon, and every evening for three weeks. He preached from the Bible and showed people the verses that impressed him that Jesus would come in 1844.

The Harmon family was excited about the meetings. "I don't want to miss a single one," Ellen said. Each day for three weeks, the family brought their lunch basket and stayed from morning until late at night.

Ellen loved the preaching, but one thing made her sad. She thought she'd been so bad God couldn't save her. "Dear Jesus," she cried quietly, "You are coming so soon. I never can be good enough to go to heaven with You. I do wrong things all the time."

Finally, she felt so sad she talked to her pastor. He patted her shoulder. "Don't worry, Ellen," he said kindly. "All you have to do is believe what God promised." He opened his Bible to 1 John 1:9 and asked her to read a promise God made for everyone.

Ellen read aloud. "If we confess our sins, he is faithful and just to forgive us our sins, and to cleanse us from all unrighteousness."

"Trust your loving heavenly Father, Ellen," the kind man said. "He loves you. He's on your side. He wants you to be saved." The Holy Spirit helped Ellen believe that Jesus had forgiven all her sins, too, and that He would save her.

Great happiness filled Ellen. A greater happiness than she'd ever known. She wanted to give her whole life to her wonderful Saviour and be baptized. On a special day, she was baptized in the rough waters of the ocean near her home.

"The waves were high and dashed on the sandy beach," Ellen said later, "but I felt as peaceful as a quiet river. Oh, what happiness! My sins were all washed away in that water. I had never felt so happy."

As she walked back up the beach after her baptism, her mother wrapped her in a blanket and a hug. "Jesus," Ellen whispered, "I belong to You. I will love You always."

Preacher William Miller continued to preach in Portland, Maine. Many people came to listen. "King Jesus is coming!" he kept telling them. "Hurry! Get ready for the great event."

Everywhere people listened. Some laughed and made fun. The people who laughed and made fun of Preacher Miller called the people who believed "Adventists."

33

That meant those people believed that Jesus' second return, or advent, was soon. The people who believed Preacher Miller truly were Adventists.

There were hundreds of thousands of advent believers. Pastors of many different churches invited *Adventists* to come and share their exciting new beliefs with their congregations. There were Lutheran Adventists, Baptist Adventists, and Methodist Adventists, but no Seventh-day Adventists—not yet.

Ellen and her family were Methodist Adventists because they belonged to the Methodist Church. They expected Jesus to come in the sky to take them back to heaven to the beautiful homes He'd prepared for them. They believed He was coming the very next year.

Satan kept tempting Ellen to think she was too wicked for Jesus to love or save. Every night, after Elizabeth fell asleep, Ellen knelt beside her bed. "Oh, Jesus, You're so perfect and holy. How can You ever save me? I do bad things every single day. How can You save me, Lord Jesus? I want to go with You so badly."

Jesus heard. He wanted Ellen to know that she was one of His precious children and how much He loved her. One night, He gave her a dream.

Ellen dreamed that she saw the door of her room open. In walked a beautiful, shining angel. He came to her and asked, "Do you wish to see Jesus? He is here."

"Oh yes!" Ellen said, jumping up out of her bed. "I'd rather see Jesus than anything in the whole world."

"Then follow me," the angel said. He led Ellen up some steps. Some steps she'd never seen before. Finally, they reached a door. The angel opened the door and motioned inside. "Go on in, little Ellen. He's here."

Ellen stepped right inside and found herself standing beside the most glorious Being she'd ever seen. Instantly, after looking into His kind eyes, she knew she stood before Jesus. King Jesus. The Ruler of the universe.

She felt so reverent she bowed down before her Saviour.

Jesus laid His hand tenderly on her head. "Don't be afraid," He said softly. The sound of His sweet voice thrilled and filled her with happiness and peace.

The angel appeared again and took her by the hand. "Come," he said, "it's time to go back." He led her back down the stairs and to her bed. Then he went back out through the door.

Suddenly Ellen awoke. She was full of joy. Jesus had smiled His beautiful smile upon her. Her fear was gone. In her happiness, she knew Jesus understood her desire to please Him. She also knew she could trust Him to save her. She fell asleep thinking of the beautiful Jesus, His tender smile and kind eyes.

The Adventist people felt so excited about Jesus' coming that they gave most of the money they had to print papers. People could then preach and give away the papers to share the great news everywhere.

Ellen, now fifteen, was eager to help spread the good news of Jesus' soon return. But she couldn't because she wasn't strong enough. In fact, at this time, she wasn't able to get out of bed. "There must be someway we can help," she told her sisters Sarah and Elizabeth. "What can we do?" The girls prayed earnestly to be able to help.

Jesus put a thought into their minds. "We'll give every cent we can earn to help tell people Jesus is coming back," they decided. "We don't need candy or toys. We won't even buy new clothes, because we won't need them after Jesus comes."

Ellen asked Papa if they could help make hats to earn money to help pay for the printing of the papers.

"I'll give you a quarter for every hat crown you weave," he answered. A crown of a hat is the part that fits on your head.

So every day, Sarah and Elizabeth came right home from school and hurried through their chores, then helped Ellen weave straw hats.

The Harmon children had gone out into the fields after the wheat had been harvested. There they gathered the long stems of wheat and straw that had been dropped on the ground. At home, they sorted the stems according to size and length so Ellen could use them.

Now Ellen's sisters soaked the straws in water overnight. The next morning, they ironed them flat so Ellen could weave them into crowns for their father's straw hats.

Sitting in her bed, Ellen could make one crown each day. She was happy to give that twenty-five cents every day to help more people learn that Jesus would soon be coming.

5

Sad and Disappointed

Mama, I've never been so happy!" Ellen exclaimed as her mother helped her into her wheelchair. "Only three more months, and Jesus will come. He's going to make me all new. Just think, Mama, He'll give me a strong, healthy body, and I'll have a beautiful face— no more smashed nose! I can hardly wait for October twenty-second to come. Oh, Mama, I love Him, I love Him, I love Him! I wish everyone in the whole world loved Him too."

Seven years had gone by since Ellen had been hit in the face with a rock. Seven years of pain. And years of sadness, too, because she wasn't strong enough to attend school.

But during those years, she'd made Jesus her best Friend. She loved to remember her wonderful dream when Jesus told her not to be afraid. And she never forgot His beautiful smile.

Ellen still made crowns for hats. As she worked in bed making the crowns, she prayed for her friends. She still gave every penny she earned to buy papers to give away telling the wonderful news she'd learned from Preacher Miller—"King Jesus is coming in less than three months. He will come in the clouds of heaven on October 22 this year! Get ready. Get ready. Get ready."

The glorious news traveled like spreading fire. Men, women, and children confessed their sins so they could be ready. Many, many people were baptized. Newspapers carried big headlines. Churches were too small to hold all the people who wanted to go to the meetings, so they met in huge tents. Every night, 5,000 people crowded into a tent that was made to hold only 4,000. People also stood around the edge listening.

Every morning when Ellen woke up, she sent her thoughts flying straight up to God.

"Take me, dear Saviour," she prayed. "Keep me from doing or saying or even thinking anything that will draw me away from You or that will hurt anyone. Make me pure and clean, Lord Jesus, just like You."

As the days went by, Ellen, Elizabeth, Robert, and Sarah kept telling each other that Jesus would be coming in a month, then three weeks, two weeks, one week, then in a few days. Excitement grew in their hearts every day.

Finally October 21 came. All that day, Ellen, Elizabeth, Robert, and Sarah kept repeating, "This is our last day on earth. Jesus is coming tomorrow!"

At the supper table, Father Harmon said, "Children, this is the last time we'll eat supper around this table. Tomorrow, we'll eat with Jesus in heaven."

Ellen was thrilled just thinking about that! Jesus coming tomorrow! Food didn't seem very interesting or important. Tomorrow, she would see her best friend, Jesus.

Night came. Even though they had a hard time going to sleep, no one had to wake up the twins the next morning. Finally, the day had arrived—October 22, 1844! They jumped out of bed before the sun even came up. They wanted to watch the sky and be the first to welcome Jesus.

A hundred thousand Adventists waited for Jesus that morning. Some gathered in churches or in homes. Others waited in fields or on a hillside.

As the Harmon family waited, they sang praises to God. They repeated His promises. They talked to Him in prayer.

Slowly, the sun crossed the sky. Jesus did not come.

"He'll be here by sunset," Ellen said. She kept waiting and hoping.

Sunset came. Darkness and night covered the earth. But Jesus still had not returned!

Tears ran down Ellen's cheeks. "Why? Papa, why didn't Jesus come?"

Papa choked back his own tears as he encouraged the family. "My dear children, we don't know why Jesus didn't come. But we know God's Word is true. We'll trust Him. Someday, we'll understand what happened."

Jesus did not come that day. Ellen, Preacher Miller, and the disappointed

Adventists had figured out from the Bible the exact day and year of the prophecy. But they didn't understand that the Bible was pointing to the time when the great judgment in heaven would begin, not to the time when Jesus would come back to earth.

Even as Ellen and the other Adventists cried and tried to understand, the angels of heaven carried Jesus to the Most Holy Room in the heavenly sanctuary. There Jesus met God, His Father, and the great judgment began. When Jesus' work is finished there, He will return, just as Ellen and her family believed He would.

6

Good News From Heaven

The days and months after the Great Disappointment were difficult for the Harmon family and the others who had planned to be in heaven. Like the Harmons, many had given all the money they had to help print the papers telling everyone to be ready to meet Jesus.

Father Harmon had to work terribly hard just to earn enough money to buy food for his family. And the people who hadn't believed made fun of them. "Never mind," Papa kept saying, "God will take care of us."

"He will!" Ellen chimed in. "He will!"

Ellen's and Elizabeth's birthdays came soon

after the Great Disappointment. On November 26, the twins turned seventeen years old.

Ellen understood why she didn't get a birthday present. Her parents had given all their money to share Jesus' coming. They'd sold everything in the house that they could get along without until Jesus came. They even sold their horse and carriage. She'd done the same thing when making her hats. No one had any money.

Ellen felt sad, not because she had no birthday gift, but because she'd been so certain she'd celebrate her seventeenth birthday in heaven with Jesus.

One day, Ellen fought to keep back her tears. She turned her face up to Him in heaven. "Dear Jesus, I love You. Please tell me why You didn't come. I know You will come someday because You have promised. Please help me be cheerful. Help me give courage to my family and friends who are sad. Thank You, Jesus. Amen."

Jesus heard Ellen, even though she was sick and could speak only in a whisper. He had plans for her, if she was only willing to work for Him.

About two weeks after the twins' birthday, one of Ellen's friends, Mrs. Haines, invited her to come spend a few days with her.

Though Ellen could hardly stand up, her mother encouraged her to go. "It'll be good for you to have a change," Mama said.

So the next morning, with a bag of clothes and her Bible on her lap, Ellen leaned forward eagerly as her brother pushed her across town in her wheelchair. Mrs. Haines was only a little older than Ellen, and Ellen knew they would have a good time together.

One morning, three of their girlfriends came to visit. They all loved God, so they read their Bibles together. "Was it really Jesus who was leading us when we thought He was coming October 22, or was it something Preacher Miller made up?" they kept asking.

"Let's ask God to help us find the answer as we study our Bibles," one of them suggested. They all knelt down so they could speak to God. Jesus was there. Ellen felt His gentle presence.

Quietly, the young women prayed together. Ellen could only speak in a whisper when her turn came. Suddenly she was silent.

She forgot she was kneeling in prayer. She forgot her friends knelt beside her. She did not know anything that was happening in the room. God was giving her a wonderful dream.

Ellen saw a bright shining angel beside her. She felt as if she were being lifted up, up, higher and higher. She turned and look down, trying to see her friends and the other Adventists. She looked everywhere and couldn't see them.

"Look again," the angel said. "Look a little higher."

Ellen looked up higher, and there she saw a narrow path going up, up, all the way up to heaven. The Adventists were walking on this path toward God's Holy City. A bright light at the beginning of the path below was shining up. It gave light for everyone's feet and kept them from stumbling and falling off the narrow path. Those who kept their eyes on Jesus did not fall, for He was leading them.

Some of the people grumbled. "I'm tired of this long, hard climb," they complained. "Jesus is not our leader."

Then the light for their feet went out, and they stumbled and fell off the narrow path into the dark world below.

Ellen saw that the Adventist people who kept their eyes on Jesus reached the beautiful sea of pure glass just outside the Holy City. She saw Jesus smile as He placed a golden crown upon the head of each person.

She saw Jesus raise His shining arm and swing open the gates, each made of one great pearl. The gates swung on their glorious hinges as Jesus called: "Come in, my children, every one of you. You've suffered for Me and sacrificed everything for Me. Come in and enjoy your heavenly home."

Ellen walked in with the others and felt so happy to be home in heaven.

Then the dream ended. Ellen woke up and found herself with her friends again in Mrs. Haines's home.

"God has answered our prayers!" she told her four friends kneeling around her. She told them about what she had seen. "We are the Adventist people climbing the narrow path to heaven. A lovely angel told me the bright light at the beginning of the path is the good news of the soon coming of Jesus. He's leading us all the way to our heavenly home."

7

The Day Ellen Ran Away

llen could hardly wait to tell her mother what had happened. As usual, Mama greeted her with a kiss. "What's happened, Ellen?" Mama asked. "You seem so happy."

"Mama," Ellen whispered. She still could not talk aloud. "Oh, Mama, Jesus gave me the most wonderful dream while we were praying. He led us to heaven, Mama. He talked to me. *To me. He talked to me.* I was right there. He showed me how it will be when He comes in the sky to take us to heaven with Him."

"My precious daughter," Mama said. "God is very near to you. He's sending a message to all of us through you. Tomorrow night, the Adventist believers meet at our house. We still don't know why Jesus didn't come October 22. We're confused, but when you tell us what God showed you, it will be like a bright light to help us understand."

Alone in her room that night, Ellen could not sleep. The thought of telling her dream to a whole group of people frightened her. "Oh, Lord," she called out, "I cannot do it. I cannot talk. I'm too young. I can't do it, Lord."

The next morning, Ellen felt even worse. "Where can I hide?" she asked herself. She forgot how her best Friend Jesus always helped her. She decided to be gone when the meeting started that evening.

Ellen ran away. She didn't really run, because she was too weak to run. Instead, she rode three miles over the snow in a sleigh to her best friend's house. Her friend was happy to see her, but she wondered why Ellen seemed so unhappy.

And so Ellen hid. But Jesus understood. He knew how shy and frightened she felt. He knew where she was hiding and sent one of the Adventist leaders to encourage her. "Ellen Harmon," he asked when he arrived, "are you doing what God wants you to do?"

Ellen knew she wasn't pleasing God. She didn't answer the man. Instead she turned, hurried upstairs, and hid in her friend's bedroom. Her eyes didn't shine now. Tears poured from them and ran down her cheeks. She truly wanted to obey God, but she felt too afraid.

The man followed Ellen up the stairs. He knocked on the bedroom door behind which Ellen hid. Tearfully, Ellen opened the door.

"Are you going to be at the meeting this evening?" he asked.

"No," Ellen answered as she shook her head.

The man looked sad. "Ellen," he said, "God has given you a message to share with all of us. We need to hear what He wants to tell us. He's using you to speak for Him. I think it's your duty to go on home." Then he turned, went downstairs, and out the front door.

"Oh, God," Ellen cried. "I can't. Father, don't leave me." Exhausted, she lay on the bed. After a long, long time and many tears, she surrendered. "God, if You give me the strength to go home tonight, I'll tell the group there about the dreams You gave me."

Ellen did get home that night, but the meeting had already ended. A few days later, the Adventists met again at the Harmon home. This time, Ellen bravely told them everything God had shown her. Those sad people were thrilled to know that Jesus was leading them, even in their disappointment.

They believed God was using Ellen as His messenger, even though she was only a teenager.

Ellen felt happy after she told the group of the special dream God had given her. She had obeyed her best Friend, Jesus.

One day, God gave Ellen another dream. The dream seemed so real Ellen thought it was truly happening.

In her dream, she stood with the Adventist people looking toward the sky. They watched a tiny cloud far, far away in the east, no bigger than a man's hand. As it came nearer, it grew larger and larger.

When the cloud came close enough, Ellen could see it wasn't a cloud at all. It was made of thousands and thousands of shining white angels! Then she heard them singing a beautiful song—an angelic song as she'd never heard before.

Above and over the cloud of angels hung a beautiful rainbow, brighter than any she'd ever seen. Suddenly, she saw Jesus! Her Jesus! The King of kings! There He sat, right in the center of the angels and the rainbow. His hair looked white and curly. Many glittering crowns sat on His head. He held a silver trumpet in one hand.

Jesus blew the trumpet, and people all around the world heard the clear, silvery tones.

Ellen and her friends trembled as they saw Jesus look right at them. "Am I ready? Am I ready?" they asked.

The angels stopped singing instantly. Not one sound could be heard in the solemn silence.

Then Jesus spoke in His wonderful voice. "Do not be afraid. I will take care of you if your hands are free from violence and your hearts are filled with love for God."

That made Ellen happier than ever. She loved God with all her heart. She had not been cruel or hurt anyone. She knew He'd forgiven and forgotten all her sins.

Again the air rang with the angels' song,

clearer than any song Ellen had ever heard. The glorious white angel cloud moved closer and closer, *but it did not touch the earth.*

Then Ellen saw something that made her even more excited. She watched as Jesus looked down at the graves of people who had died loving and obeying Him. She heard His trumpet-clear voice call, "Awake! Awake My people, you who sleep in the dust, arise!"

Then a mighty earthquake shook the earth. Graves opened all around the world, and all of God's people came up from their graves. Alive! Strong! Beautiful! Ellen and her friends recognized some of the people they knew. Everyone shouted, "Alleluia! Praise our God!"

Soon they saw bright shining angels carry tiny babies and little children to their mothers and fathers, who held them close and hugged them in their arms.

Then Ellen felt something happening to her own body. Her thin, sickly body changed before her eyes into a strong, beautiful body that would never, never be sick again. She glanced around and saw that everyone had strong new bodies—bodies that would never be sick, never be hurt, never, ever die.

Ellen looked around to see everyone as excited as she. Everyone busily tried to take in the marvelous things happening around them. She stood up and jumped. She felt as steady as a tree. She spun around. Still she felt strong with no pain. Oh, Jesus was wonderful.

Then suddenly Ellen felt her feet leave the ground. She felt herself rising into the air. She looked around and saw her friends and the other Adventists rising with her. Everyone was rising!

Ellen knew it was Jesus' strong, matchless love that pulled them right up off the ground into the air. Jesus wanted them all to be with Him *now and forever.*

Ellen watched as she and the others rose to join Jesus in the cloud of angels. Right away, they joined the angels in singing songs of praise to Jesus. For seven days, they traveled with Jesus through the sky on their way to the homes Jesus had prepared in heaven.

Ellen's dream was so real it seemed to her that it was really happening. Even though she was sad when it ended, she knew that someday it would happen just the way she had seen it.

8

Messenger for God

One night, God sent an angel to talk to Ellen. He told her that God wanted her to do a special work for Him. He wanted her to be His messenger.

"Your life as a messenger for God will not be easy," the angel said. "You must write down whatever God shows you. You must tell people His words. You must travel wherever He needs you to go. Some people will hate you. Many will tell lies about you. Do not be afraid. God's everlasting love will be with you. He will give you strength. If you are ever in danger, just pray, 'Lord, send another angel.' He will, and you will have two angels to keep you safe."

The thought of talking to the Adventists in her own parents' home had frightened Ellen. The thought of traveling away from home and having people hate her and lie about her terrified her. But this time she didn't run away. Instead, she dropped to her knees to talk to God.

"Lord, dear Lord," she began, "I love You, but You know I can't travel. This is the middle of winter. Everything's all frozen outside. And besides, Lord, how can I write when my hand shakes so badly I can't even hold a pen? And what if I become proud and sinful? Please, please, ask someone else to be Your messenger."

The only thing Ellen heard was the angel's words, "Make known to others what I have shown you."

Ellen went to her father and told him all that had happened. "Papa," she cried, tears streaming down her cheeks, "I want to obey God, but how can I?"

"Ellen, my child," he said, reaching strong arms around her thin body, "if God asks you to talk, He'll give you back your voice. If He asks you to travel, He'll give you the strength.

If He asks you to write, He'll guide your trembling hand. Don't be afraid, Ellen. You must trust Jesus. He'll never ask you to do anything that's impossible."

A few days later, the Adventists met at the Harmon home again to study and pray. Father Harmon told them about Ellen's struggle.

"Let's pray for her," someone said. Ellen knelt with them. As she heard their prayers, she felt braver. Silently in her heart, she felt willing to do anything for Jesus. "Yes, Lord, I'm Yours. I'll do anything You ask."

At that very moment, a bright light shone on Ellen. For a moment, she saw and felt angels surrounding her. "Tell others what I have shown you," she heard them repeat.

"I will. Yes, dear Jesus, I'm willing to do whatever You ask me. Anything! Anything with Your help."

Ellen's friends were still kneeling, all except one older man who couldn't kneel because of the pain in one knee, but God let him see something exciting anyway. "I saw a ball of fire come down from heaven," he called out. "It struck Ellen on the heart. I saw it! I saw it! I'll never doubt her again."

The ball of fire was God's way of sending the Holy Spirit to her and showing her that He'd accepted her as His messenger.

That very same week, Sam, Ellen's sister Mary's husband, stopped to say Hello to the family. Sam and Mary lived thirty miles away in the city of Poland. Before Sam left, he told Ellen that Mary wanted her to come visit them for a few days when the weather improved.

Immediately, Ellen remembered God wanted her to travel for Him. "I can go now, Sam," she said.

"Now?" Sam asked, surprised. "It's bitter cold, and all I have is an open sleigh."

"I promised Jesus I'd go anywhere, anytime," Ellen said. "I'll go with you now."

Mother Harmon fixed a quick lunch and heated some bricks. Then they tucked Ellen into the sleigh with lots of blankets and the bricks to heat her little tent formed by the blankets.

For thirty miles, the horses pulled them over the frozen snow. At last, they reached Sam and Mary's place.

A few days later, Mary took Ellen to talk to a group of disappointed Adventists. Ellen knew God wanted her to tell them about the beautiful vision-dreams Jesus had given her.

Bravely, she stood up, but when she tried to speak out, her voice wouldn't work. She didn't give up. Not Ellen. She began by whispering her words. The people leaned forward to hear her. Suddenly, her voice came out loud and clear.

She talked to the people for two hours. She told about Jesus leading the disappointed Adventists up the long path and also about the glorious time when Jesus comes down from heaven to take His children back to heaven with Him.

After Ellen finished speaking, the people had many questions. Ellen gladly answered each one; then she sat down. Right away, her voice was gone, and she could only speak in whispers again.

Ellen's heart filled with peace. She knew God had used her as His messenger to bring hope to His people on earth.

9

Ellen Sees the New Earth

Ellen had never felt happier than after she told the believers about her dreams. She had done what God wanted her to do.

But some Adventists didn't believe God really talked to Ellen. "Don't believe a word Ellen Harmon says," they said. "Satan gives her those dreams. God could never use someone who didn't finish even fourth grade."

Other people said, "How wicked of her to say that God speaks to her. It's the devil, not God."

When Ellen heard these terrible lies, she felt sad. She wanted people to like her just as much as anyone does. It hurt her even worse when some of her friends began to wonder if her dreams were from Satan.

She felt so sad she got very sick. Her parents asked other Adventists to come pray for her. They knelt around her bed and asked God to make her well.

And He did! He healed her instantly! Everyone felt the Holy Spirit in the room.

The next moment, He gave Ellen another vision right there in front of her friends.

"Glory! Glory! Glory!" Ellen's voice rang out. She no longer saw the people around her in the room. Instead, she felt herself surrounded with the brilliant light of God and holy angels. Then she found herself in heaven with Jesus and many angels.

But her friends in the room were still watching her. Her eyes were wide open, and she never blinked. Sometimes, she spoke to someone they couldn't see. Although they couldn't see what Ellen was seeing or hear what Ellen was hearing, they noticed something else right away.

"She's not breathing," someone whispered. "Look!"

"That's right," Father Harmon said. "Ellen

never takes a single breath while she is seeing God's vision. This is one way that we know her visions come from God. God keeps her alive even though she doesn't breathe."

"Thank You, God," one of them prayed out loud, "for allowing us to see Ellen while she is having a vision."

"Now we know we can trust Ellen," another said. "Now we know that her dreams come from God."

Meanwhile, Ellen was seeing heaven. And Jesus.

"Follow Me," Jesus called. Ellen and all the people and angels followed Him down through the skies to the earth. The moment Jesus' feet touched the top of a mountain, it divided right in half. The two sides moved away until there was a wide, flat plain in front of them.

"Look up!" several voices called.

Ellen looked and saw the glorious Holy City, the New Jerusalem. "The city, the great city!" everyone called. "It's coming down from God out of heaven."

"Come," Jesus said, as the city settled down onto the plain. "Come with Me. I'll show you the new earth where you will live."

They followed Him and soon discovered He'd changed this old world into a beautiful new earth. He'd even made beautiful country homes for His people. Some people went into their new homes, took off their crowns, and laid them on golden shelves.

Then they went outside to care for their gardens. A brilliant light shone around their heads, and they sang joyful songs of praises to God. Ellen looked around and saw no ugly weeds in the gardens. So no one had to pull them. None of the plants had thorns to hurt fingers, either. And there weren't even any harmful insects that would eat or ruin the beautiful vegetables and flowers.

"Come now and see My holy temple on Mount Zion," Jesus called. Immediately, everyone followed Him. Ellen walked along and picked fragrant flowers. "They will never fade," she sang.

They passed a field of tall green grass. The breeze waved it back and forth ,making it look like gold, then like silver. *How proudly it waves to King Jesus*, Ellen thought.

As they walked on, Ellen was thrilled with

one wonderful sight after another. She saw great lions and tiny lambs resting side by side on the tender green grass. Leopards and wolves played together, and some of the animals walked beside them.

Mount Zion was just in front of them, and the glorious temple was on top of it. Seven hills nearby were covered with brightly colored roses. Ellen saw little children climb or use their wings to fly to the top of the hills to pick the never-fading flowers.

Jesus showed them His glorious temple . Then He left and went back to the Holy City. "Come, My people," He soon called. "You have suffered for Me. You have done My will. You have been faithful. Come, eat the supper I have ready for you. I will serve you."

"Alleluia! Alleluia! Glory!" Ellen shouted with the others as they made their way to Him. The dining table, made of silver, stretched out for many miles. But with her newly made eyes, Ellen could see from one end to the other.

Colorful fruit covered the table—grapes, figs, pomegranates, peaches, cherries, strawberries, and every other kind of fruit. High piles of almonds and other nuts added to the beautiful sight. Everything looked so delicious!

It looked far better than any food Ellen had ever seen. "Please, may I have some fruit?" she asked Jesus.

He looked at her with His loving smile. "Not now, Ellen. Anyone who eats the fruit of heaven does not go back to earth. But, Ellen, if you're faithful, it won't be long until you will eat fruit from the tree of life. Ellen, I need you to go back to earth and tell people there what I have shown you."

An angel took her in his arms and carried her gently back to this earth. Then she felt herself take a long breath.

The others in the room noticed it too. "Look, she's beginning to breathe." As they watched, Ellen took another breath and then another as her empty lungs filled with air.

Ellen glanced around the room. It seemed so dark after seeing the light of heaven. She could barely see the people there. "It's dark," she murmured. "So dark."

Finally her eyes adjusted to the dim light, and she smiled at her mother and friends.

"Ellen," Mother Harmon asked, "can you

tell us anything that Jesus showed you just now?"

"I'll try," Ellen said. "But there are no words on earth good enough to describe the glorious things I've seen." She eagerly told them all about the things Jesus had shown her.

Whenever God gave Ellen a vision, He controlled her body as well as her mind. One time, in front of an audience, God gave Ellen a vision. As before, she forgot all about the people in front of her. She just stood there with her hands folded.

Two men in the group didn't believe in Ellen's vision. They started making fun of her.

"Go up and try to pull her hands apart," someone else called out. So they went up on the stage to try. But as hard as they pulled, they could not move her hands apart.

"Maybe you could move her fingers," another person suggested. Once again, the two men tried. But they could not even move one finger.

Ellen was still in her vision. She raised up both her arms and slowly waved them.

"Try to stop her arms from moving,"

others suggested to the two men. "Hold them still." Each man grabbed one of Ellen's small wrists. With their powerful arms, they could not keep her arms from moving.

When the vision ended, Ellen did not know what had happened. But her wrists, where the men had grabbed them, were not even a little sore.

10

Every Drop of Water in the Ocean

One afternoon, the Lord spoke to her. "Ellen, I need you to be in Portsmouth, New Hampshire, tomorrow."

"Yes, Lord," she said. "I meant it when I promised to go anywhere and do anything for You." Then she remembered He'd said tomorrow. "Tomorrow, Lord? It's sixty miles to Portsmouth, and I don't have any money to buy train tickets for Sarah and myself."

Then she remembered to trust Him. "But I know You'll work it out, Lord, so I'll leave it to You. I'm thankful Sarah's always willing to leave her work and go with me. One more thing, Lord. I know You'll give me the strength and a loud-enough voice to speak Your messages."

The next morning, Ellen and Sarah packed clothes for their trip. Sarah wondered how they'd pay for their train tickets. "Don't you worry about that," Ellen said. "God has it all figured out."

Just then, they heard a noise outside and saw a strange man driving a wagon right up to their gate. He rushed to the open door. "I've been impressed that someone here needs money. Is that right?" he asked, all out of breath.

Ellen told him about their trip. The man reached into his pocket and gave them enough money to cover all their expenses. "Come get into my wagon, and I'll take you to the station."

As they rode, he told them he'd come twelve miles to bring them the money. "My horse raced all the way," he added. "I couldn't hold him back." Ellen glanced at the horse and saw it was covered with sweat.

When they reached the station, the man helped the girls from the wagon into the train. "Thank you, sir. God bless you," was all they had time to say before the train jerked to a start.

As the girls sat comfortably in the train, they talked about how God had cared for every single thing. "All we have to do is relax and let God take charge," Ellen said. "He knows how better than anyone."

After Ellen's eighteenth birthday, she heard about an Adventist family living on an island. These people felt disappointed and discouraged because Jesus hadn't come.

"I want to visit them and tell them God loves them," Ellen said. "Today."

Mr. Gurney, who was visiting the Harmons, offered to borrow a sailboat from a friend and take Ellen there. He did, that very same day. Sarah went also.

The blue sky, the deeper blue water, and the smooth, peaceful ocean made Ellen feel calm and happy. After a while, the sun sank behind the ocean, turning the sky and water many shades of pink.

But a little later, black clouds hurried across the sky until they covered it. Then lightning began to flash, and thunder roared into their ears. Soon the waves grew huge and wild. Rain poured into the boat too, and it rolled from side to side. Ellen and the others were soon soaked. "Are we going to sink?" Ellen cried.

Mr. Gurney shook his head. "I can't hear you," he yelled into the wind. "I can't control the boat in this wind—and I don't know where we are."

Ellen felt terrified. No one knew they'd be sailing that day, so no one would be looking for them to help them. "God, help us!" she finally screamed. "No one knows where we are. Send us help, Father!" The wind snatched the words from her mouth almost before she screamed them.

Mr. Gurney couldn't hear her, but God could. Right there in that sailboat with lightning flashing, thunder roaring, and rain pouring, He sent Ellen a vision.

Suddenly, Ellen didn't hear the storm anymore. All she heard was the quiet voice of Jesus. "Ellen," He said, "don't be so frightened. Trust Me, Ellen. I won't let anything happen to you. I'd dry up every drop of water in the ocean before I'd let harm come to you."

"Why?" Ellen screamed into the wind.

"Why?" He repeated. "Because your work for Me has just begun."

Ellen didn't hear Him anymore, and the short vision ended. She heard the storm roaring over her again and felt the pouring rain, but all her fear had vanished. She hurried to tell Mr. Gurney that they'd be safe.

The storm continued, but they were no longer afraid. "Let's call for help together," Mr. Gurney said after a while. "Maybe someone on the island will hear us."

So they did. "Help! Help! Help!" they shouted over and over together.

A little girl in the house nearest to the shore couldn't sleep. The loud storm had kept her awake. Suddenly, she sat up in bed. "Did I hear someone call?" she asked herself. Then she heard it again. Her father had rescued many ships in danger, so she ran into his room and called him.

He listened a moment, then jerked on his raincoat. "I'm coming!" he yelled as he lighted a lantern and rowed out into the darkness.

Shouting back and forth, they finally found each other. The man tied a rope to the sailboat and towed it to shore. Just as Ellen and the others left the boat, the rope broke, and the sailboat headed out to sea. "Forget the boat," the man said. "It's gone."

He took them to the nearby home of the Adventist family they'd come to visit. The mother brought robes for Ellen and the others and hung their clothes beside the warm fire to dry. Then they brought them hot bowls of soup. Ellen thought she'd never tasted such good food in her life.

They spent most of the night singing to God and praising Him for His wondrous way of saving them from the storm. The discouraged Adventist family they'd come to encourage felt God's presence in the rescue, too, and felt excited to know that God still cared for each of them in every little way.

The next morning, the men walked around the island looking for the sailboat but didn't find even a piece of sail. "The boat's at the bottom of the ocean," they said sadly.

The man they'd been visiting said he would take them home in his sailboat.

As they sailed over the smooth water, they neared the place where they had borrowed the boat. *How can we pay the owner for his lost boat* they wondered.

"I'll have to stop singing and preaching," Mr. Gurney said. "I'll go back to my black-smithing and pay every cent I can on the boat until it's paid for."

"I have five dollars at home," Sarah said. "It'll help a little."

At first, Ellen didn't say anything, because she didn't have any money to give. Then she finally said, "God kept us from drowning. He sent us on this trip. Somehow, He'll help us pay for the sailboat so we can still keep working for Him. Let's ask Him."

While the gentle waves lapped their boat, they asked God to help them find ways to pay for the lost boat. They prayed aloud for a few minutes; then everyone prayed silently.

Soon they neared the boat owner's home. "Dear Lord," Mr. Gurney prayed out loud, "give me wise words to tell my friend what happened. Thank You, Lord."

As they neared the empty dock where the boat had been kept, Ellen saw something! She pointed, and they all talked at once. "Look! Look! It can't be! This is impossible!"

But it was there! The sailboat they'd lost at sea was tied to the dock. Not even a sail was torn.

The owner approached. Mr. Gurney pointed at the boat. "How did that get here?" he asked.

"I thought you returned it," the owner said. "It was here early this morning."

They shook their heads, and all tried to tell the man what happened. They had many questions they couldn't answer. Who kept the boat from being broken into pieces? Who guided it out of the storm safely to its own dock? Who knew where it belonged?

But they really knew the answers. God cared for the boat and brought it home safe and sound. "He really cares about every little thing in our lives," Mr. Gurney said.

"And He wants us to spend our time working for Him," Ellen added, "not working for money to pay for a lost boat."

11

Ellen's Second Angel

*T*wo or three time each week, Bill Jordan and his sister, Sarah, visited the Harmon home in Portland to study and pray with them.

"We have an idea," Bill exclaimed one evening when they arrived. "I borrowed a horse and sleigh from a young Adventist preacher in Orrington. It's a hundred miles from here, and Sarah is going with me to return it. Ellen, why don't you go with us? You could share the good news God is giving you with the disappointed Adventists there. We could stay and travel with you from place to place."

Though so weak she could hardly speak

above a whisper, Ellen knew God wanted her to go. Hadn't she promised Him she'd go anywhere He called? Hadn't He promised He'd send a second angel if she ever needed one?

Trusting God, Ellen told the Jordans that she would go with them. Dressed in her warmest clothes, covered with buffalo robes, Ellen stayed warm as the horse pulled the sleigh across the frozen snow at a quick trot.

The trip took several days. As they rode along, Bill and Sarah told Ellen about their young preacher friend, James White. "He lives on a farm with his parents," Bill said. "James taught over a thousand people to know Jesus and to believe in His return before the disappointment. Now he's searching for answers about why Jesus didn't come so he can explain the mistake to them."

James White met the travelers when they reached Orrington. The Jordans told James that Ellen was going to speak that very evening to a group of Adventists in their home. James decided to stay and see what this young woman would say.

That evening, what he saw and heard convinced him that Ellen was a messenger from

God. "Every Adventist must hear this wonderful news," he exclaimed. He looked at Ellen. He could see that she was young and shy and had no money. "How do you plan to travel as you spread this good news? How will you get from group to group?"

Ellen shook her head and smiled. "I have no idea how I'll travel, but God always opens a way."

"I know what we'll do," James said eagerly. "I'll drive my horse and sleigh and take you and the Jordans to visit the Adventist groups. I know many of them. They need encouragement. I'll send notices ahead and organize meetings."

For nearly three months, James White drove Ellen and the Jordans hundreds of miles, stopping at Adventist homes. Ellen told each group about the visions God had given her. Her message brought joy and courage to those who listened.

Not all the Adventists welcomed Ellen. Some had very strange ideas. One group read in the Bible, "Unless you change and become like little children, you'll never enter heaven" (Matthew 18:3).

"We must act like little children," they preached. So instead of walking like adults, they crawled on their hands and knees. They hid behind doors and peeked out. They even sucked their fingers. People who acted strangely like this were called fanatics.

Ellen tried to explain to them that Jesus meant they should be pure, innocent, kind, and obedient like little children. But the fanatics wouldn't listen. Instead, they screamed loudly so no one could hear Ellen. They shouted hateful words at her. They even tried to drive her out of their town.

Ellen kept praying, "Lord, send my second angel to me." And God always did. Ellen was not attacked or hurt.

The weather grew warmer, and as the snow melted, James couldn't drive his sleigh anymore. They arrived back in Orrington exhausted from months of traveling.

Friends of the Jordans had invited the travelers to their home for a few days. The weary travelers looked forward to the quiet rest. But when they arrived, the woman grabbed them and jerked them into the house. "Get in quickly," she said. Then she slammed the door and locked it.

"What's going on?" Bill Jordan asked.

"The police are blaming Ellen for all the trouble and noise the fanatics are making," the hostess said. "They've made a law that no Adventists may meet together to pray, no matter how few. If they're found, they'll be thrown into jail. Some Adventists have given up believing there is a God, but many others are faithful, yet lonely and filled with terror."

"Oh," Ellen said, "they need help. We must meet with them this very night and give them courage. God's promise of protection is for them too."

Secret messages went out for anyone who wished to come and meet with Ellen. Late that night in total darkness, Ellen told about the wonderful visions the Lord had given her about the glories of heaven and the new earth. She also made sure everyone understood that Jesus loved them and still led them. Everyone left feeling happier and blessed by God.

Suddenly, God gave Ellen a vision. He told her that she must leave Orrington early the next morning because an angry mob of men planned to harm her. The moment James

White heard about God's warning, he went into action. How could he help her? He couldn't use his sleigh now that the snow had melted. If he could borrow a rowboat and find two strong men to help, they could row Ellen and the Jordans to the seaport town of Belfast. Then he could put them on a steamship headed for their home in Portland, Maine.

"I'll do it!" he said aloud.

Before the first light of morning, the group silently climbed into the rowboat. With the oars, the two men pushed the boat away from the bank. They sailed down the river as the new day dawned with a beauty that told them God was near, guarding them with His love.

When they reached Belfast, Ellen and the Jordans boarded a passenger ship ready to sail for Portland. Ellen stood on the dock waving her thanks to the young man she'd grown to admire—the young man God had sent to protect her while she traveled. The tall young man, James White, stood on the shore waving as if he couldn't stop.

Ellen wondered how long it would be before she saw the earnest Christian young man again.

Only a few weeks after Ellen arrived safely at home, God asked her to visit other Adventist groups in New Hampshire. As soon as James learned Ellen and her sister Sarah were traveling, he left at once to find them. He felt that God had given him the job of protecting Ellen.

James told Ellen and Sarah some tough men had given him a horsewhipping and thrown him into jail overnight after he'd helped Ellen escape. "I'm so glad it was me instead of you," he told Ellen. "A beating like that would have killed you."

As they worked together, James and Ellen grew fond of each other. But they believed Jesus would come that very year and thought they shouldn't marry. God knew their thoughts, so He talked with Ellen in a vision. He told her He wasn't coming right away and that she could trust James White always and completely.

"You know what this means?" James said, his eyes shining. "It means He wants us to marry. We'll both be happier that way, and you'll always have me to protect you."

"James, I must hear from God before

making such a serious decision," Ellen said. "Let's each pray about it earnestly for two weeks." James agreed.

Then one day which they would never forget, James stopped at the Harmon home. Ellen welcomed him. They talked about other things until James could wait no longer. "Shall we marry?" he asked.

Ellen looked directly into his loving eyes. "Yes, James. Yes."

On August 30, 1846, James Springer White, twenty-five years old, and his bride, Ellen Gould Harmon, eighteen, stood before a justice of the peace in Portland, Maine, and promised to love and be faithful to each other. They both knew that their promises were to each other and to God.

For the next thirty-five years, James and Ellen worked together for God. They helped start the worldwide Seventh-day Adventist Church, a church that will last until Jesus comes.